DEVIN JOHNSTON

TRAVELER

DEVIN JOHNSTON WAS BORN IN
1970 AND SPENT HIS CHILDHOOD
IN NORTH CAROLINA. HE WORKS FOR
FLOOD EDITIONS, AN INDEPENDENT
PUBLISHING HOUSE, AND TEACHES AT
SAINT LOUIS UNIVERSITY IN MISSOURI.

ALSO BY DEVIN JOHNSTON

[POETRY]

Sources   Aversions   Telepathy

[PROSE]

Creaturely and Other Essays

*Precipitations: Contemporary American
Poetry as Occult Practice*

TRAVELER

TRAVELER

DEVIN JOHNSTON

FARRAR, STRAUS AND GIROUX

NEW YORK

FARRAR, STRAUS AND GIROUX
18 West 18th Street, New York 10011

Published in 2011 by Farrar, Straus and Giroux
First paperback edition, 2013

The Library of Congress has cataloged
the hardcover edition as follows:
Johnston, Devin.
    Traveler / Devin Johnston. — 1st ed.
    p. cm.
    ISBN 978-0-374-27933-2 (cloth : alk. paper)
    I. Title.

PS3610.O385 T73 2011
811'.6—dc22

2011008457

Paperback ISBN: 978-0-374-53348-9

Designed and composed by Quemadura

www.fsgbooks.com
www.twitter.com/fsgbooks
www.facebook.com/fsgbooks

P1

CONTENTS

The lines of this new song are nothing
But a tune making the nothing full . . .

LOUIS ZUKOFSKY

TRAVELER

FROM MEDICINE LODGE

From Medicine Lodge
to Coldwater, from Coldwater
to Protection and beyond,
this undulating line
intersects no industry
yet slows to Central,
resumes a bare number,
and finally frays
in shallow tracks
where Black Kettle
and Standing Feather
took their geologic time
and left no cairn.

Salt and gypsum collapsed
to form a basin
shadows race across,
their smooth momentum
broken only
by a spindly windmill

with its corrugated trough
or scratchy, windrattled
cottonwood, a graph
of fluctuating force,
anything upright
under revision.

A twist of hair
threads the ring
of a dried-up sink
as stackenclouds and fibrous
sonderclouds draw silver
from common sagebrush,
or waneclouds streak
the afternoon with grains
of polished wood—
only to kindle flame
as everything shuts down
but cloudworks, unfinished
parts of a world.

NOTHING SONG

after William IX, Duke of Aquitaine

I made this up from nothing.
It's not myself I sing,
or love, or anything
    that has a source.
I dreamed these words while riding
    on my horse.

I've neither youth nor age.
Ambitions out of range,
I feel no joy or rage
    to see them go.
One midnight worked the change
    that made me so.

I wonder, do I wake
from dreams, or dream I wake?
Beneath a sheet, I shake
    and clutch my heart,
though part of me—aloof, opaque—
    remains apart.

For such uncertainty
I've found no remedy
in psychotherapy
    or sedatives.
I rummage through debris
    where nothing lives.

A friend I've never met,
unknown to me as yet,
has kindled no regret
    or happiness,
no tender sobriquet
    to curse or bless.

As coldly radiant
as stars, and light-years distant,
this expectation can't
    embrace a life,
but shines on, ignorant
    of lust and strife.

My song of nothing done,
I ride from Avignon
and leave my words to one
    who turns a key
to find the deadbolt drawn
    and stable empty.

EXPECTING

what will she
now a she

trailing clouds
yet hearing our

muffled voices
all the while

from this dark
world and wide

what will she
mew or bray

as any envoy
might derive

an embryon
from animal

or amnion
from tender lamb

though tethered to
a human form

an embryon
in amnion

or bloom of jellies
at the whim

of storm and tide
the ocean's roar

above, around,
and then inside

AUBADE

A vacant hour
before the sun—
and with it a valve's
pneumatic hush,
the deep and nautical
clunk of wood,
chanson du ricochet
of rivet gun,
trowel tap,
and bolt drawn—

the moon sets
and water breaks.

Curled within
a warm pleroma,
playing for time,
you finally turn
and push your face

toward November's
glint of frost,
grains of salt,
weak clarities
of dawn.

CESAREAN

Graphing pain,
the toco monitor
scrolls a white
bounding line
on a blue field:
not heraldry but
a lightning flash
illuminates
the rugged range
of your estate,
from deep crevasse
to trackless slopes
of Traversette.
Dryly tapping,
a clerical ghost
prints a pan-
oramic strip.
In a sudden charge,
the air contracts
a vast expanse

(remote and thin)
to this bare room
where surgeons cut
a Gordian knot
and everyone
says *wonderful*
when they forget.

TRAVELER

From the foot of Cotopaxi
and across the Gulf

a Blackburnian warbler
follows a pulse,

follows Polaris
and the Pole's magnetic field

through travail
and travel's long ordeal,

until he drops
to a black walnut's
pinnate leaves

tossing like waves
in the North Sea

and glances toward
my lamplit, stationary world
of smooth planes:

against a cloud,
his throat's flame.

FOREIGN OBJECT

The hours spent on transpacific flights
pass like a sandstorm through the Mongol steppes,
lodging a single grain—an irritant
to memory—within the furrowed cortex.
Nacred by revolving doubt, it grows
a pearl as black as the ocean depths
and lustrous as the moon
through sublimated ice.

This pearl outlives its host—and can be bought
in Shanghai, from an unassuming shop
on the French Concession's western edge.
The jeweler plucks it from a velvet box
and cups the pearl like a Dramamine
in the hollow of her outstretched palm.
She stands like that, expectantly,
revolving shapes to come.

ROGET'S THESAURUS

At the first surge of psychotic trance,
to ward it off or ride it out,
Peter Roget took up a list:
breeds of dogs, human bones, anatomies
of cloud, or forms of transport.
It steadied his mind to study the spokes
of wheels glimpsed through vertical slats:
van, wagon, whisky, tumbrel, truck;
the blur of whips and hooves,
ornate signage stripped of syntax.

Now, among aseptic cells
of Bonne Terre, Roget's thesaurus
circulates more than Malcolm X.
One offender, stout as a mule,
circles the yard while leafing through
a dog-eared passage (cf. *trough*)
from *hole* to *eye* to *aperture* and on:
outlet, inlet, orifice, throat,

channel, chimney, pit, pore,
sieve, riddle, borer, screw,
bodkin, needle, warder, gouge.

As an officer calls for head count,
the morning sun reticulates
filigree of chain link
and a curl of concertina wire.
It glances off the hubcap
of a distant Cadillac
joining the flow of traffic.

NOWHERE

Sifu John has left the dojo
and struck out on his own.
No more shit from Master Jong,
no endless adjudications
of single whip, no banquets,
belts, dues, or membership.

His only student—big dude
with the tight, slick ponytail
of Steven Seagal—
got lit and locked
a bartender in tiger claw,
then spent a night in jail.

Clearly distinguish
empty from full,
the classics instruct.

Mornings, feeling thick, John
crosses off his mother's list

at Schnucks, returning home
with tourniquets of plastic bags.

Evenings, sifu and student
grasp the sparrow's tail
beside a picnic pavilion
perched above the park's basin,
its pooling shadows
emptied of pedestrians.

As snow begins to fall,
they return to fundamentals
of *Peng, Lu, Ji, An* . . .
slow as three-toed sloths
under the orange glare
of sodium lights
with all else thrown in darkness.
Getting nowhere.

SET APART

Set apart
from the compound
friction of forest,
a rough-barked
bur oak,
mostly trunk,
outlives
its understory.

A sapling in 1700,
it rose like smoke
from leaf litter,
a totem for those
who told tales
vertically,
every episode
the offspring
of earth and sky.

Carotenoids flare
through its vascular system
in slow time,
releasing aromas
of black tea
and tobacco.

Winter-hardened,
the oak endures,
a column supporting
nothing but its own
fixed extension.

The fine point
of a feeding warbler—
a drifting spark
or cursor—
ghosts its crown.

COLD-BLOODED

Beyond a ring
of mercury light
nothing conspicuous
could survive
the coming night.
The rippling hunch
of a barred owl
propounds as yet
no prey, no rattle
in late September's
coil of fern.
A cold breath
of Brush Creek
gently rocks
joe-pye weed,
but skin still
radiates heat
from the setting sun.
Fever kindles
a turbulent flow

continuous with sleep,
shape-shifting
until an earthen
effigy uncurls
its cursive form
across the ridge.
The snake god
swallows an egg
as Draco slips
through tattered leaves.
Beyond the creek,
a white truck
catches the last
light of day
and sends it back.

HIGH AND LOW

Placid Pan
snores in the sun
as a thunderhead
comes to rest
on the canyon's rim.
From a hump
of high withers
a ridge descends
to a moist rhinarium
or the puckered phrase
e pluribus unum.

Bison bison,
periodic
        as prairie fire,
graze its aftermath
of new grass,
their burnt heads
slung low
and panicked by any

cracked report.
The lightning bolt,
lord of everything,
drawn on a skull
in red ochre,
draws a herd
whose delicate hooves
thunder to raise
a cloud of dust.

STORM AND STURGEON

When a thunderstorm
      trundles down the Wabash,
revealing the form
      of flow in every flash,
northerlies lash
      the walls that keep us warm,
rummaging grass,
      scattering flock and swarm.

Beneath an icy
      column thick as phlegm,
this cold coyote
      of our river system
peers through a scrim
      of silt and leaf debris
as lightning skims
      the shoals of Harmonie.

As each percussion
     shakes the sturgeon's bladder—
a loose vibration
     felt in fleshy matter—
her switch-tail stirs
     beds of hibernation,
bottom dwellers
     lost in cloud formations.

TANGLED YARN

Darner, sewing needle,
exclamation damsel,

pennant, flying adder,
tang- or sanging eater,

fleeing eather, bluet,
steelyard, spindle, booklet,

skimmer, scarce or common,
sand or shadow dragon,

cruiser, shadow damsel,
devil's horse or saddle,

darning needle, dancer,
meadow hawk or glider,

water naiad, threadtail,
sylph or sprite or penny nail.

THE INLAND ROAD

Wake up, wake up,
a kettle yawns
and coughs,
slurring its copper bell
with faint
horns.
Haru-ichiban
with winter gone
clicks
a sharp stick
on walls of stone
and shuffles off
a slough
of plastic sheets.
Somewhere below, a horse
stamps at his trough
and rattles empty stirrups.

EARLY APRIL

Under the Sinclair's brontosaurus sign,
three men collect around a coffeepot
on metal folding chairs. One talks
of rust on a spring-tooth harrow, matters
of cultivation, while the others
ruminate on plastic mugs. Down Route M,
the lek returns to a low ridge
of soy and hissing fescue, booming grounds
abandoned to the long nose of a tractor
where only roans had cast a shadow.

Tympanuchus cupido taught Lakotas
how to dance, its throat patch yellow
as egg yolks, its booming glug
of a low tone swallowed, head feathers erect
in practiced threat. Desire's kettledrum.
Theirs is a culture more intractable
than forbs or Scottish fiddle tunes.

A county south, at Adam-ondi-Ahman,
Mormons wait in a canvas blind
as fog lifts from combed furrows
for a Clovis Christ to come. If he does,
they'll send him up a tree to scout
what's rushing across the low ridge,
whether prairie chicken or machine.
Both live forever until they die.

MARCO POLO

As dusk turns to dark, swallows turn to bats:
their smooth parabolas of flight erode
to flutters. Emitting dry clicks above
the peak of what we hear, they probe
for moth wings. Perched in her high chair,
my daughter echoes the names of things
in early Mandarin or Cantonese.
Each syllable returns—without its edge
of consonants—to test the contours of
a human face. As blue turns to black,
the neighbors' children shout *Marco! Polo!*
in antiphony across the swimming pool,
the sightless id calling to its ego,
groping toward a mark beyond the pale.

Riding through the Gashun Gobi desert
in search of Kublai Khan, a traveler might
nod off and veer from his companions, hearing
voices or the clatter of caravans
through the dark, across the scalloped dunes,

as particles collide in booming sands.
If he follows, dreaming, woe betide him.
So the Mongols fasten little bells
around the necks of camels, goats, and mules.
Their ringing rides along with us like stars.

AT SEA RANCH

Like cordage from a lost rig,
a loose braid of bullwhips
breaches a wave, holdfast
anchors adrift, canopy ripped.
Bladder wrack or black tang
wraps a hollow bulb,
and from each terminal, a stipe
curls in Arabic script.

Darkness can't descend
but rises off the sand,
rising up like fine smoke.
As the tide flows in,
living bullwhips drown
and leave the wrack afloat.

ORACLE BONES

In subdivisions of the dead
a Plum Blossom cigarette
stuck upright
in fresh dirt
glows in a gust of wind.

Counterfeit passports,
subway tickets,
spirit transfers
to offshore accounts,
official chops
for disappearing ink,
paper currency
bearing the watermark
Bank of Heaven, Ltd.,
all burn
for otherworldly use.

Pulling weeds
at the edge of darkness,

trustees undertake
burdens of ownership
as Shang diviners
busy themselves
with hairline cracks
in oracle bones,
ox scapulae
and turtle shells,
filing reports
and currying favor.

Umbrellas open
around an excavation
and all of this world
pours into the next.

THIN PLACE

White ash,
you wait for me

as I will wait
for someone.

What but skin
feels the wind,

what darkness
makes distinctions?

Breaking down
dusk and dawn,

housewreckers
on horse scaffolds

syncopate
their hammers.

Brick dust
drifts like smoke,

tents of habitation
withdrawn,

hinges of habit
undone.

RELATIVES

no one left
the same to say

what it is
that changed

APPETITES

1

My daughter, three, lies awake
talking in confidential tones
with one she calls
my friend who eats me.
Its very name raises the question
of where to draw a line
in affinities and affections.
Like a brook, her voice
burbles down the hall,
on and on, a lilt
of barely suppressed delight.

2

Mrs. Rondinella drifts
six feet above her shadow
in a buoyant chaise longue,
eyes shut in quiet bliss,
fingers interlaced
below her navel.
She has a baby growing
in her belly, I explain.
Squinting at the sun,
you speculate,
She swallowed it?

3

Ravenous for each other,
a teenage couple intertwine
in a darkened carport,
eyes shut in concentration,
tongue exploring tongue,
tooth scraping tooth,
on and on, each attuned
to the faint taste
of aluminum;
appetites unslaked.

KID

Before I've shed my scarf and coat,
she's on me, shouting *Kid! We're late!*
Like surf, she batters around my knees,
aggressive joy, insistent need.
Her greeting, mock-tyrannical,
initiates a game or spell,
though one as lightly taken up
as any blossom she begs to clip
and later begs to cast aside.
Hey kid! she crows, and I accede
to misrule—*kid* assumes a force
by which familiar roles reverse.
Outside, a mockingbird explodes
in hectic song, its vocal raids
on chickadee and chimney swift.
We hurry past to catch a flight
to some fantastic Bangladesh,
our destination crudely sketched
in chalk, a scratchy pictograph

of crocodile or banyan leaf.
Invention lags, the day turns cold,
and we resume accustomed roles.

At dusk, while her authority
gives way to sleep, I watch TV:
A Buddhist lama passed away
and left his pupil, Tenzin-Ja,
to scour the land for his rebirth.
The lama's silk hat pointed north
and a giant, star-shaped fungus bloomed
beside the northern wall of his tomb.
Such omens guided Tenzin-Ja
to where a scraggy hamlet lay
like scree beneath its granite slope.
An old man drove a herd of goats
through the gate on which his child
swung at play, the arcing ride
from help to hindrance back to help.
Presented with a row of bells,
the boy, as if awakening
from deep in a trance, grasped and rang
the lama's own. *It's mine, it's mine!*

—a glint of something in his eye
that set his family ill at ease.
So Tenzin-Ja took custody
of the rinpoche who once raised him,
exchanges signaled by a chime.

ROUGH PATCH

You can tell, by symptoms of neglect,
something of his circumstance:
the chipped and buckled eaves, deflated
jack-o'-lantern beside the stoop,
an ember under snow,
or red ants swarming the sill,
crossing a line of cinnamon
in some far-flung military action.
You can tell, by frying onions,
their thick domestic weather,
or the grim satisfaction with which
his vacuum overlooks
a plain of fur and dust.
I can tell from a little
just what a whole lot means.
You treat me like somebody
you ain't never seen.

Hackle stacker, mayfly cripple,
and Bloom's parachute ant

crowd an ashtray—to rarify
the quality of failure.
Mornings, a frowzy Manx
kneads his chest with claws unsheathed,
thrumming with desire
and contempt in equal measure.
Every other weekend, he rolls out
a court-appointed cot
from the closet for his daughter.
You can feel, with your fingertips
against his metal door,
vibrations from the interstate
or seismic evidence
of Furry Lewis,
circa 1928.

CRUMBS

1

You could caulk every crack
and mice would still find ways
through our foundation, sleep
would still get broken,
and we would still
be sweeping up the floor.

2

A hen pecks
the kitchen step
for scratch,

fluffs against
the damp chill,

and scrapes her beak
like a struck match
along the sill.

3

Out of the frozen bed,
a curl of carrot leaf.

Out of sleep, a hand
slides between the sheets.

STATIC

Zipping your skirt, you rustle past,
sand hissing through a glass,
with the bedouin snap and flash
of static-electric
sparks disturbing fabric.
This morning's charge could rouse
The Desert Fathers of Sinai
over which I drowse.

A LOST NOTEBOOK

after Propertius

So my little notebook is gone,
and with it a thousand things I'd written!
Smears from the heel of my hand
authenticate the source, unsigned.
It knew how to please a girl in my absence,
and how, when I would stray,
to turn a soothing phrase.
No split calfskin made it precious:
we're talking college-ruled and spiral-bound.
Whatever the bond, it always procured
the right effect, and always kept its word.

Left on the dining-room table, my notebook
often accreted this sort of thing:
I'm angry you showed up late yesterday.
Did you find someone more lovely?
Or do you intend to fling
a trumped-up charge in my face?
Or else, her looping hand announced,

You'll come today, we'll skip our classes
and mingle on my bed for hours,
and whatever else a keen girl
invents to win an assignation.

What misery! Some frugal bastard
keeps accounts on its blank pages
and shelves it with *The Millionaire Next Door.*
I'll offer a bounty for safe return:
Who'd cling to pulp in lieu of cash?
Hurry, kid, go staple this
to a telephone pole, and indicate
that the owner lives on Sidney Street.

THE YOUNG PRETENDER

Though living in a foreign land,
I recognize my avatars
in every song the washers sing:
the cuckoo is a bonny bird;
my moorhen has feathers enew;
there was a man came from the moon.
But none could recognize a king
who buys his butter on the street
and brings it home in a lettuce leaf.
All the while, I have in mind
a clachan where we passed the night:
sleet against a cottage roof,
a flight of warblers on the pipes,
and dawn before I thought upon
the road, skirting mountains black
beneath a cloud, but silver-laced
with forces where the sun broke through.
By simple reckoning—though math
is not my strength—at twenty-five
I set my foot against the main

with seven true companions
and seized through sheer exuberance
what twenty French battalions
never could. My standard raised
a skirling clan from every bit
and cities fell without a shot.
For seven months I saw through steel
and made it melt, a brain of fire
with feet of ice. Then Culloden:
my skin still prickles at the name.
I sat astride a gray gelding—
a net of lemons slung across
my saddlebow—and stuck a sprig
of Highland heather in my cap
beside the Stuarts' white cockade.
I heard my own high, lisping voice
shout, as from a long way off,
Go on my lads! The day is ours.
What a fool—the heights of young
ambition come to broken eggs.

BURREN

The wisp I once pursued
would utter, drunk or high,
an accusatory *you*
or proud, emphatic *I*,
returning quietly
at break of day to bed
and the old, familiar *we*
she carries in her head:
a village on the crest
of Turlough Hill, a ring
of huts now dispossessed
of any moving thing.
A toppled cairn has wrung
another paradox
of blood from stone and hart's tongue
from grikes in pavement blocks.
Amid dry-stone dikes
of endless iteration—
meanders, copes, and heights
of tireless variation—

a Holstein turns her gaze
from human artifacts
to contemplate the maze
of her digestive tract.
Across the karst from Black Head
and south to Mullach Mór,
sedimental slabs embed
a teeming ocean floor.
Stone from blood: a bluff
arisen from the sea
compressed its lacy cuff
in fossil memory.

IONA

Arriving damp with sea spray, fingers cold,
I disembark a day already old
as billows scatter seeds or smithy sparks
across the west, against the growing dark
of Dalriada, Pictland, Gododdin,
and Strathclyde, shadows flooding every glen.

Birds take flight from nested hierarchies
of class, order, family, genus, species,
in and out of weeks, across an ocean,
skimming foamy paragraphs of Ossian,
an immram of uncertain end or goal
until the island rises from a shoal.

Columbidae *Columba livia*
sails on outstretched wings from its armada,
catching sudden flame above the firth
and coasting down like Lucifer toward earth
in trumpet spirals, forms that wind and rain
erode from standing stone and souterrain.

Driven off its course, a tousled heron
drags the night behind it like a curtain
and sinks its toes in a hag of sphagnum moss
beside a ringing river. With a toss
and muffled flap, this pilgrim smoothes its plume
and gingerly advances through the gloom.

Eyeing fingerlings beneath a ledge,
the heron whets its gaze on the water's edge.
Its neck, now limp as rope, abruptly bows
and floats a sleeky head above the flow
as in a cobra's hypnotized display.
With a sudden thrust, the bird impales its prey.

Fluid rock, Iona wraps in mist
the island's endless morphogenesis:
addenda, curling up the crust of land,
and corrigenda, subsidence of sand;
addenda, beech and hazel, oak and ash,
by corrigenda burn to smoke and ash.

Gleaned from shafts of sunlight, barley grain
steeps in a tank of Lochan Torr and rain,
the kernels dried in ovens, milled to grist,

oared to mash, the wort drawn off and mixed
with yeast in wooden washbacks, boiled until
its spirit fogs the neck of a copper still.

Heaven blends with Hell. The whisky bears
a nose of salt and peat reek, earth and air.
It warms the belly, blooms, and stimulates
a lucid dream as it evaporates,
pissed away against a public wall
beneath the stars, as summer turns to fall.

In winter, clouds haul water from its source,
the ocean basin, welling up by force
of deep convection through the troposphere
to irrigate the crops and kailyards here,
propelled by the polar jet from trough to trough
across the rippled flats and furrowed crofts.

Kings of the present world, your glories fail,
your frigates founder in a sudden gale:
here lies the *Swan*'s gigantic, bony hull
submerged in silt beneath the Sound of Mull,
a reef for conger eels to colonize,
her ribs dismantled by the rushing tides.

Light rain sifts from clouds in which it's bound
instead of breaking loose to drench the ground:
mammato-cumuli distend like udders,
braiding rills that feed the Forsa's waters.
From smoking haar to affluence to loch,
this long hydraulic cycle never stops.

Masses coalesce as planets, flung
through empty space and spinning round the sun
by force of gravitation while we sleep,
the piles of consciousness embedded deep
in Tertiary basalt, gneiss, and schist.
To such foundations Columkill is fixed.

Not far beneath the surface, all who died
sustain the darkness, cloistered from the sky.
In slow combustion, corpses decompose,
stripped by slugs of feathers, fur, and clothes;
of flags of disposition, yours and mine;
of family, genus, species, kith, and kind.

Of all the dead, not one can read our psalter,
An Cathach, borne through clashing swords—the Battler!
Locked in a cumdach forged from plates of brass,

its leaves have caked and cockled, gone to grass,
and yet its songs still circulate as sound,
escaping spiral form and snapping hound.

Pursuing my own thoughts along a track
across the rocky headland Ardmeanach,
I found a basalt frieze of fossil leaves
and frozen force of trunk in low relief.
This tree outlasted Vikings, Picts, and Jutes,
transformed, but still remembering its roots.

Quarried blocks of Ben More set in stone
the legend of a dead volcanic cone.
Who heard its molten lava hiss and sing,
extruding through the crust to which it clings?
What buzzard climbed a sgurr of ashen air?
What Moses grasped the glyphs eroded there?

Returning day, volcanic spilth of dawn,
instantly overflows the Firth of Lorn:
dies irae, day of humid chill,
a day of knuckles cracking, snow on sill,
a day to counteract a night of love.
From sleep's edge I feel a gentle shove.

Sunlight beams across this beehive cell:
a socket for the skull, a hissing shell
or cochlea, inverted coracle,
it amplifies the laughter of a gull.
This blank stone on which a blanket curled
has heard confession from a savage world.

The ferry sounds its horn, a tuba blown
by Israfel to roust these weary bones.
Illumined limbs untangle, creases fade,
extremities revive. Having strayed
all night, my thoughts return along a strand
of *Helix* snail shells pulverized to sand.

Venus greets the morning sun as Lucifer,
struck against Iona's rocky spur.
Orion slipped the Outer Hebrides
four months ago and left the Pleiades
a fading smudge of fingerprint on steel.
Such tropes revolve like spokes within a wheel.

X-rays pierce a silver Tompion
pocketwatch recovered from the *Swan*:
beneath a calcite crust and hunter case

the sun and moon sit frozen on its face.
Time has stopped. Beleaguered Jacobites
still crouch in caves, arrested in their flights.

"Ye'll Aye Be Welcome Back Again," a reel,
meanders through the Bellachroy Hotel:
hung over or reprised from Friday night,
it emanates from sources out of sight.
On flute and fiddle, fingers leap like deer;
My heart's in the Highlands, my heart is not here.

Zealous dukes and earls have cleared the way
for blackface sheep to trample Torosay
as clachan cedes its place to congregation,
cliff to cloud, and rupture to abrasion.
Flocks disperse from pens; the days unfold
between volcanic heat and glacial cold.

THE ROUGH BOUNDS

I like the sort of track that passes
out of English altogether
as through the Bronze Age bowl
of Glen Moidart, its edges cracked
by forces flooding the drove road
with *wee lochans*. Each excerpts
from sgurrs of Dhomhuill Beag
and Dhomhuill Mór and heaps of Norn
rimmed with mud. The wind whirples
leaf from branch where seven beeches
make a stand. Beyond a white bull
that bears the head of Constantine,
the Coffin Road branches off
to Eilean Fhianain, Finan's Isle
(if road can ever reach an island).
Keep straight, until your tracks
disperse in streams and soggy moss
like final whispered wisps of smouk.
Where you stop, a fald of stane
has folded up its last sheep.

ACKNOWLEDGMENTS

These poems have previously appeared in
*Alhambra Poetry Calendar, The Baffler,
Colorado Review, 52nd City, Free Verse,
The Hat, The Nation, Notre Dame Review,
The Paris Review, Poetry, Poetry Daily,
The Washington Post Book World,* and
on poets.org. "The Young Pretender" was
published as a broadside by Woodland Pattern
Book Center in Milwaukee. I am grateful
to the Howard Foundation for support
during the completion of this book.

feminine gospels

Carol Ann Duffy

feminine gospels

poems

FARRAR, STRAUS AND GIROUX

NEW YORK

Farrar, Strauss & Giroux
18 WEST 18TH STREET, NEW YORK 10011

COPYRIGHT © 2002 BY CAROL ANN DUFFY

ORIGINALLY PUBLISHED IN 2002 BY PICADOR, AN IMPRINT OF PAN MACMILLAN LTD,
    GREAT BRITAIN
PUBLISHED IN 2003 IN THE UNITED STATES BY FABER AND FABER, INC.
FIRST AMERICAN PAPERBACK EDITION, 2005

THE LIBRARY OF CONGRESS HAS CATALOGED THE HARDCOVER EDITION AS FOLLOWS:
DUFFY, CAROL ANN.
    FEMININE GOSPELS : POEMS / CAROL ANN DUFFY.   1ST ED.
       P.   CM.

    1. WOMEN   POETRY. I. TITLE.
    PR6054.U38F46 2003
    821'.912–DC21

                                                        2003040886

ISBN: 978-0-571-21130-2
ISBN: 0-571-21130-5

WWW.FSGBOOKS.COM

P 1

for my brothers –

Frank, Adrian, Eugene and Tim

Contents

Acknowledgements

Poetry Review; *The Rialto*;
The Times Literary Supplement; Waterstones;
The Year of the Artist / Wolverhampton City Council;
BBC Radio.

Carol Ann Duffy gratefully acknowledges a NESTA Fellowship.

feminine gospels

The Long Queen

The Long Queen couldn't die.
Young when she bowed her head
for the cold weight of the crown, she'd looked
at the second son of the earl, the foreign prince,
the heir to the duke, the lord, the baronet, the count,
then taken Time for a husband. Long live the Queen.

What was she queen of? Women, girls,
spinsters and hags, matrons, wet nurses,
witches, widows, wives, mothers of all these.
Her word of law was in their bones, in the graft
of their hands, in the wild kicks of their dancing.
No girl born who wasn't the Long Queen's always child.

Unseen, she ruled and reigned; some said
in a castle, some said in a tower in the dark heart
of a wood, some said out and about in rags, disguised,
sorting the bad from the good. She sent her explorers away
in their creaking ships and was queen of more, of all the dead
when they lived if they did so female. All hail to the Queen.

What were her laws? *Childhood*: whether a girl
awoke from the bad dream of the worst, or another
swooned into memory, bereaved, bereft, or a third one
wrote it all down like a charge-sheet, or the fourth never left,
scouring the markets and shops for her old books and toys –
no girl growing who wasn't the apple of the Long Queen's eye.

Blood: proof, in the Long Queen's colour,
royal red, of intent; the pain when a girl
first bled to be insignificant, no cause for complaint,

and this to be monthly, linked to the moon, till middle age
when the law would change. *Tears*: salt pearls, bright jewels
for the Long Queen's fingers to weigh as she counted their sorrow.

Childbirth: most to lie on the birthing beds,
push till the room screamed scarlet and children
bawled and slithered into their arms, sore flowers;
some to be godmother, aunt, teacher, teller of tall tales,
but all who were there to swear that the pain was worth it.
No mother bore daughter not named to honour the Queen.

And her pleasures were stories, true or false,
that came in the evening, drifting up on the air
to the high window she watched from, confession
or gossip, scandal or anecdote, secrets, her ear tuned
to the light music of girls, the drums of women, the faint strings
of the old. Long Queen. All her possessions for a moment of time.

The Map-Woman

A woman's skin was a map of the town
where she'd grown from a child.
When she went out, she covered it up
with a dress, with a shawl, with a hat,
with mitts or a muff, with leggings, trousers
or jeans, with an ankle-length cloak, hooded
and fingertip-sleeved. But – birthmark, tattoo –
the A-Z street-map grew, a precise second skin,
broad if she binged, thin when she slimmed,
a precis of where to end or go back or begin.

Over her breast was the heart of the town,
from the Market Square to the Picture House
by way of St Mary's Church, a triangle
of alleys and streets and walks, her veins
like shadows below the lines of the map, the river
an artery snaking north to her neck. She knew
if you crossed the bridge at her nipple, took a left
and a right, you would come to the graves,
the grey-haired teachers of English and History,
the soldier boys, the Mayors and Councillors,

the beloved mothers and wives, the nuns and priests,
their bodies fading into the earth like old print
on a page. You could sit on a wooden bench
as a wedding pair ran, ringed, from the church,
confetti skittering over the marble stones,
the big bell hammering hail from the sky, and wonder
who you would marry and how and where and when
you would die; or find yourself in the coffee house

nearby, waiting for time to start, your tiny face
trapped in the window's bottle-thick glass like a fly.

And who might you see, short-cutting through
the Grove to the Square – that line there, the edge
of a fingernail pressed on her flesh – in the rain,
leaving your empty cup, to hurry on after
calling their name? When she showered, the map
gleamed on her skin, blue-black ink from a nib.
She knew you could scoot down Greengate Street,
huddling close to the High House, the sensible shops,
the Swan Hotel, till you came to the Picture House,
sat in the musty dark watching the Beatles

run for a train or Dustin Hoffman screaming
Elaine! Elaine! Elaine! or the spacemen in 2001
floating to Strauss. She sponged, soaped, scrubbed;
the prison and hospital stamped on her back,
the park neat on her belly, her navel marking the spot
where the empty bandstand stood, the river again,
heading south, clear as an operation scar,
the war memorial facing the railway station
where trains sighed on the platforms, pining
for Glasgow, London, Liverpool. She knew

you could stand on the railway bridge, waving
goodbye to strangers who stared as you vanished
into the belching steam, tasting future time
on the tip of your tongue. She knew you could run
the back way home – there it was on her thigh –
taking the southern road then cutting off to the left,
the big houses anchored behind their calm green lawns,
the jewels of conkers falling down at your feet,

then duck and dive down Nelson and Churchill
and Kipling and Milton Way until you were home.

She didn't live there now. She lived down south,
abroad, en route, up north, on a plane or train
or boat, on the road, in hotels, in the back of cabs,
on the phone; but the map was under her stockings,
under her gloves, under the soft silk scarf at her throat,
under her chiffon veil, a delicate braille. Her left knee
marked the grid of her own estate. When she knelt
she felt her father's house pressing into the bone,
heard in her head the looped soundtrack of then –
a tennis ball repeatedly thumping a wall,

an ice-cream van crying and hurrying on, a snarl
of children's shrieks from the overgrown land
where the houses ran out. The motorway groaned
just out of sight. She knew you could hitch
from Junction 13 and knew of a girl who had not
been seen since she did; had heard of a kid who'd run
across all six lanes for a dare before he was tossed
by a lorry into the air like a doll. But the motorway
was flowing away, was a roaring river of metal
and light, cheerio, au revoir, auf wiedersehen, ciao.

She stared in the mirror as she got dressed,
both arms raised over her head, the roads
for east and west running from shoulder
to wrist, the fuzz of woodland or countryside under
each arm. Only her face was clear, her fingers
smoothing in cream, her baby-blue eyes unsure
as they looked at themselves. But her body was certain,
an inch to the mile, knew every nook and cranny,

cul-de-sac, stile, back road, high road, low road,
one-way street of her past. There it all was, back

to front in the glass. She piled on linen, satin, silk,
leather, wool, perfume and mousse and went out.
She got in a limousine. The map perspired
under her clothes. She took a plane. The map seethed
on her flesh. She spoke in a foreign tongue.
The map translated everything back to herself.
She turned out the light and a lover's hands
caressed the map in the dark from north to south,
lost tourists wandering here and there, all fingers
and thumbs, as their map flapped in the breeze.

So one day, wondering where to go next,
she went back, drove a car for a night and a day,
till the town appeared on her left, the stale cake
of the castle crumbled up on the hill; and she hired
a room with a view and soaked in the bath.
When it grew dark, she went out, thinking
she knew the place like the back of her hand,
but something was wrong. She got lost in arcades,
in streets with new names, in precincts
and walkways, and found that what was familiar

was only facade. Back in her hotel room, she stripped
and lay on the bed. As she slept, her skin sloughed
like a snake's, the skin of her legs like stockings, silvery,
sheer, like the long gloves of the skin of her arms,
the papery camisole from her chest a perfect match
for the tissuey socks of the skin of her feet. Her sleep
peeled her, lifted a honeymoon thong from her groin,
a delicate bra of skin from her breasts, and all of it

patterned A to Z; a small cross where her parents' skulls
grinned at the dark. Her new skin showed barely a mark.

She woke and spread out the map on the floor. What
was she looking for? Her skin was her own small ghost,
a shroud to be dead in, a newspaper for old news
to be read in, gift-wrapping, litter, a suicide letter.
She left it there, dressed, checked out, got in the car.
As she drove, the town in the morning sun glittered
behind her. She ate up the miles. Her skin itched,
like a rash, like a slow burn, felt stretched, as though
it belonged to somebody else. Deep in the bone
old streets tunnelled and burrowed, hunting for home.

Beautiful

She was born from an egg,
a daughter of the gods,
divinely fair, a pearl, drop-dead
gorgeous, beautiful, a peach,
a child of grace, a stunner, in her face
the starlike sorrows of immortal eyes.
Who looked there, loved.

She won the heart
of every man she saw.
They stood in line, sighed,
knelt, beseeched *Be Mine.*
She married one,
but every other mother's son
swore to be true to her
till death, enchanted
by the perfume of her breath,
her skin's celebrity.

So when she took a lover, fled,
was nowhere to be seen,
her side of the bed unslept in, cold,
the small coin of her wedding ring
left on the bedside table like a tip,
the wardrobe empty
of the drama of her clothes,
it was War.

A thousand ships –
on every one a thousand men,
each heaving at an oar,

each with her face
before his stinging eyes,
her name tattooed
upon the muscle of his arm,
a handkerchief she'd dropped once
for his lucky charm,
each seeing her as a local girl
made good, the girl next door,
a princess with the common touch,
queen of his heart, pin-up, superstar,
the heads of every coin he'd tossed,
the smile on every note he'd bet at cards –
bragged and shoved across a thousand miles of sea.

Meanwhile, lovely she lay high up
in a foreign castle's walls, clasped
in a hero's brawn, loved and loved
and loved again, her cries
like the bird of calamity's,
drifting down to the boys at the gates
who marched now to the syllables of her name.

Beauty is fame. Some said
she turned into a cloud
and floated home,
falling there like rain, or tears,
upon her husband's face.
Some said her lover woke
to find her gone,
his sword and clothes gone too,
before they sliced a last grin in his throat.

Some swore they saw her smuggled
on a boat dressed as a boy,

rowed to a ship which slid away at dusk,
beckoned by the finger of the moon.
Some vowed that they were in the crowd
that saw her hung, stared up at her body
as it swung there on the creaking rope,
and noticed how the black silk of her dress
clung to her form, a stylish shroud.

Her maid, who loved her most,
refused to say one word
to anyone at any time or place,
would not describe
one aspect of her face
or tell one anecdote about her life and loves.

But lived alone
and kept a little bird inside a cage.

*   *   *

She never aged.
She sashayed up the river
in a golden barge,
her fit girls giggling at her jokes.
She'd tumbled from a rug at Caesar's feet,
seen him kneel to pick her up
and felt him want her as he did.
She had him gibbering in bed by twelve.

But now, she rolled her carpet on the sand,
put up her crimson tent, laid out
silver plate with grapes and honey, yoghurt,
roasted songbirds, gleaming figs, soft wines,
and soaked herself in jasmine-scented milk.

She knew her man. She knew that when
he stood that night, ten times her strength,
inside the fragrant boudoir of her tent,
and saw her wrapped in satins like a gift,
his time would slow to nothing, zilch,
until his tongue could utter in her mouth.
She reached and pulled him down
to Alexandria, the warm muddy Nile.

Tough beauty. She played with him
at dice, rolled sixes in the dust,
cleaned up, slipped her gambling hand
into his pouch and took his gold, bit it,
Caesar's head between her teeth.
He crouched with lust. On her couch,
she lay above him, painted him,
her lipstick smeared on his mouth,
her powder blushing on his stubble,
the turquoise of her eyes over his lids.
She matched him glass for glass
in drinking games: sucked lemons, licked
at salt, swallowed something from a bottle
where a dead rat floated, gargled doubles
over trebles, downed a liquid fire in one,
lit a coffee bean in something else, blew it,
gulped, tipped chasers down her throat,
pints down her neck, and held her drink
until the big man slid beneath the table, wrecked.

She watched him hunt. He killed a stag.
She hacked the heart out, held it,
dripping, in the apron of her dress.
She watched him exercise in arms.
His soldiers marched, eyes right, her way.

She let her shawl slip down to show
her shoulders, breasts, and every man
that night saw them again and prayed
her name. She waved him off to war,
then pulled on boy's clothes, crept
at dusk into his camp, his shadowed tent,
touched him, made him fuck her as a lad.
He had no choice, upped sticks,
downed tools, went back with her,
swooned on her flesh for months,
her fingers in his ears, her kiss
closing his eyes, her stories blethering
on his lips: of armies changing sides,
of cities lost forever in the sea, of snakes.

*   *   *

The camera loved her, close-up, back-lit,
adored the waxy pouting of her mouth,
her sleepy, startled gaze. She breathed
the script out in her little voice. They filmed her
famous, filmed her beautiful. Guys fell
in love, dames copied her. An athlete
licked the raindrops from her fingertips
to quench his thirst. She married him.
The US whooped.

They filmed her harder, harder, till her hair
was platinum, her teeth gems, her eyes
sapphires pressed by a banker's thumb.
She sang to camera one, gushed
at the greased-up lens, her skin investors' gold,
her fingernails mother-of-pearl, her voice
champagne to sip from her lips. A poet came,

found her wondrous to behold. She married him.
The whole world swooned.

Dumb beauty. She slept in an eye-mask, naked,
drugged, till the maid came, sponged
at her puffy face, painted the beauty on in beige,
pinks, blues. Then it was coffee, pills, booze,
Frank on the record-player, it was put on the mink,
get in the studio car. Somebody big was watching her –
white fur, mouth at the mike, under the lights. *Happy
Birthday to you. Happy Birthday, Mr President.*
The audience drooled.

They filmed on, deep, dumped what they couldn't use
on the cutting-room floor, filmed more, quiet please,
action, cut, quiet please, action, cut, quiet please,
action, cut, till she couldn't die when she died,
couldn't get older, ill, couldn't stop saying the lines
or singing the tunes. The smoking cop who watched
as they zipped her into the body-bag noticed
her strong resemblance to herself, the dark roots
of her pubic hair.

*   *   *

Dead, she's elegant bone
in mud, ankles crossed,
knees clamped, hands clasped,
empty head. You know her name.

Plain women turned in the streets
where her shadow fell, under
her spell, swore that what she wore
they'd wear, coloured their hair.

The whole town came
to wave at her on her balcony,
to stare and stare and stare.
Her face was surely a star.

Beauty is fate. They gaped
as her bones danced
in a golden dress in the arms
of her wooden prince, gawped

as she posed alone
in front of the Taj Mahal,
betrayed, beautifully pale.
The cameras gibbered away.

Act like a fucking princess –
how they loved her,
the men from the press –
Give us a smile, cunt.

And her blue eyes widened
to take it all in: the flashbulbs,
the half-mast flags, the acres of flowers,
History's stinking breath in her face.

The Diet

The diet worked like a dream. No sugar,
salt, dairy, fat, protein, starch or alcohol.
By the end of week one, she was half a stone
shy of ten and shrinking, skipping breakfast,
lunch, dinner, thinner; a fortnight in, she was
eight stone; by the end of the month, she was skin
and bone.

       She starved on, stayed in, stared in
the mirror, svelter, slimmer. The last apple
aged in the fruit bowl, untouched. The skimmed milk
soured in the fridge, unsupped. Her skeleton preened
under its tight flesh dress. She was all eyes,
all cheekbones, had guns for hips. Not a stitch
in the wardrobe fitted.

       What passed her lips? Air,
water. She was Anorexia's true daughter, a slip
of a girl, a shadow, dwindling away. One day,
the width of a stick, she started to grow smaller –
child-sized, doll-sized, the height of a thimble.
She sat at her open window and the wind
blew her away.

       Seed small, she was out and about,
looking for home. An empty beer bottle rolled
in the gutter. She crawled in, got drunk on the dregs,
started to sing, down, out, nobody's love. Tiny others
joined in. They raved all night. She woke alone,
head splitting, mouth dry, hungry and cold, and made
for the light.

She found she could fly on the wind,
could breathe, if it rained, underwater. That night,
she went to a hotel bar that she knew and floated into
the barman's eye. She slept for hours, left at dawn
in a blink, in a wink, drifted away on a breeze.
Minute, she could suit herself from here on in, go
where she pleased.

      She stayed near people,
lay in the tent of a nostril like a germ, dwelled
in the caves of an ear. She lived in a tear, swam
clear, moved south to a mouth, kipped in the chap
of a lip. She loved flesh and blood, wallowed
in mud under fingernails, dossed in a fold of fat
on a waist.

      But when she squatted the tip of a tongue,
she was gulped, swallowed, sent down the hatch
in a river of wine, bottoms up, cheers, fetched up
in a stomach just before lunch. She crouched
in the lining, hearing the avalanche munch of food,
then it was carrots, peas, courgettes, potatoes,
gravy and meat.

      Then it was sweet. Then it was stilton,
roquefort, weisslacker-käse, gex; it was smoked salmon
with scrambled eggs, hot boiled ham, plum flan, frogs'
legs. She knew where she was all right, clambered
onto the greasy breast of a goose, opened wide, then
chomped and chewed and gorged; inside the Fat Woman now,
trying to get out.

The Woman Who Shopped

went out with a silver shilling, willing to buy, bought
an apple, red as first love's heart, bright as her eye,
had plenty of change, purchased a hat with a brim,
walked with a suitor under its shadow, ditched him;

saved up a pound, a fiver, a tenner, haggled the price
of a dancing dress down to a snip, spent the remainder
on shoes, danced from the house down the street, tapped
to the centre of town where the sales had commenced,

applied for a job for the wage and the bonus, blew it
on clothes; wanted a wedding, a wedding dress, groom,
married him, wanted a honeymoon, went on one,
looked at the gold of her ring as it flashed in the sun;

flew away home to furnish each room of the house,
shuffle his plastic with hers, deal them out in the shops
for cutlery, crockery, dishwashers, bed linen, TV sets,
three-piece suites, stereos, microwaves, telephones,

curtains and mirrors and rugs; shrugged at the cost,
then fixed up a loan, filled up the spare room with boxes
of merchandise, unopened cartons, over-stuffed bags;
went on the Internet, shopped in America, all over Europe,

tapping her credit card numbers all night, ordering
swimming pools, caravans, saunas; when they arrived,
stacked up on the lawn, she fled, took to the streets,
where the lights from the shops ran like paint in the rain,

and pressed her face to the pane of the biggest and best;
the happy shoppers were fingering silk, holding cashmere
close to their cheeks, dancing with fur; she slept there,
curled in the doorway, six shopping bags at her feet.

*   *   *

Stone cold when she woke, she was stone, was concrete
and glass, her eyes windows squinting back at the light,
her brow a domed roof, her thoughts neon, flashing on
and off, vague in the daylight. She seemed to be kneeling

or squatting, her shoulders broad and hunched, her hands
huge and part of the pavement. She looked down. Her skirts
were glass doors opening and closing, her stockings were
moving stairs, her shoes were lifts, going up, going down:

first floor for perfumery and cosmetics, ladies' accessories,
lingerie, fine jewels and watches; second for homewares,
furniture, travel goods, luggage; third floor for menswear,
shaving gear, shoes; fourth floor for books, toyland,

childrenswear, sports; fifth floor for home entertainment,
pianos, musical instruments, beauty and hair. Her ribs
were carpeted red, her lungs glittered with chandeliers
over the singing tills, her gut was the food hall, hung

with fat pink hams, crammed with cheeses, fruits, wines,
truffles and caviar. She loved her own smell, sweat and Chanel,
loved the crowds jostling and thronging her bones, loved
the credit cards swiping themselves in her blood, her breath

was gift wrapping, the whisper of tissue and string, she loved
the changing rooms of her heart, the rooftop restaurant
in her eyes, the dark basement under the lower ground floor
where juggernauts growled, unloading their heavy crates.

The sky was unwrapping itself, ripping itself into shreds.
She would have a sale and crowds would queue overnight
at her cunt, desperate for bargains. Light blazed from her now.
Birds shrieked and voided themselves in her stone hair.

Work

To feed one, she worked from home,
took in washing, ironing, sewing.
One small mouth, a soup-filled spoon,
life was a dream.

                    To feed two,
she worked outside, sewed seeds, watered,
threshed, scythed, gathered barley, wheat, corn.
Twins were born. To feed four,

she grafted harder, second job in the alehouse,
food in the larder, food on the table,
she was game, able. Feeding ten
was a different kettle,

                              was factory gates
at first light, oil, metal, noise, machines.
To feed fifty, she toiled, sweated, went
on the night shift, schlepped, lifted.

For a thousand more, she built streets,
for double that, high-rise flats. Cities grew,
her brood doubled, peopled skyscrapers,
trebled. To feed more, more,

she dug underground, tunnelled,
laid down track, drove trains. Quadruple came,
multiplied, she built planes, outflew sound.
Mother to millions now,

                              she flogged TVs,
designed PCs, ripped CDs, burned DVDs.
There was no stopping her. She slogged
night and day at Internet shopping.

                              A billion named,
she trawled the seas, hoovered fish, felled trees,
grazed beef, sold cheap fast food, put in
a 90-hour week. Her offspring swelled. She fed

the world, wept rain, scattered the teeth in her head
for grain, swam her tongue in the river to spawn,
sickened, died, lay in a grave, worked, to the bone,
her fingers twenty-four seven.

Tall

Then, like a christening gift or a wish arriving
later in life, the woman had height, grew tall,
was taller daily.

> Day one saw her rising at 8 foot
bigger than any man. She knelt in the shower
as if she were praying for rain. Her clothes
would be curtains and eiderdowns, towels and rugs.

Out. Eye-high with street lamps, she took a walk
downtown. Somebody whooped. She stooped,
hands on both knees,

> and stared at his scared face,
the red heart tattooed on his small chest. He turned
and fled like a boy.

> On. A tree dangled an apple
at bite-height. She bit it. A traffic-light stuttered
on red, went out. She lit it. Personal birds
sang on her ears. She whistled.

> Further. Taller
as she went, she glanced into upper windows
in passing, saw lovers in the rented rooms
over shops, saw an old man long dead in a chair,
paused there, her breath on the glass.

She bowed herself into a bar, ordered a stiff drink.
It came on the rocks, on the house. A drunk
passed out or fainted. She pulled up a stool, sat
at the bar with her knees

                                    under her chin, called
for another gin, a large one. She saw a face, high
in the mirror behind the top shelf. Herself.

Day two, she was hungover, all over, her head
in her hands in the hall, her feet at the top
of the stairs, more tall.

                         She needed a turret,
found one, day three, on the edge of town, moved in,
her head in the clouds now, showering in rain.

But pilgrims came –
small women with questions and worries, men
on stilts. She was 30 foot, growing, could see for miles.

So day six, she upped sticks, horizon-bound
in seven-league boots. Local crowds swarmed
round her feet, chanting.

                         She cured no one. Grew.
The moon came closer at night, its scarred face
an old mirror. She slept outdoors, stretched
across empty fields or sand.

The stars trembled. Taller
was colder, aloner, no wiser. What could she see
up there? She told them what kind of weather
was heading their way –

dust storms over the Pyramids,
hurricanes over the USA, floods in the UK –
but by now the people were tiny

and far away, and she
was taller than Jupiter, Saturn, the Milky Way. Nothing
to see. She looked back and howled.

She stooped low
and caught their souls in her hands as they fell
from the burning towers.

Loud

Parents with mutilated children have been turned away from the empty
hospital and told to hire smugglers to take them across the border to
Quetta, a Pakistani frontier city at least six hours away by car.

(Afghanistan, 28 October 2001)

The News had often made her shout,
but one day her voice ripped out of her throat
like a firework, with a terrible sulphurous crack
that made her jump, a flash of light in the dark.
Now she was loud.

Before, she'd been easily led,
one of the crowd, joined in with the national whoop
for the winning goal, the boos for the bent MP, the cheer
for the royal kiss on the balcony. Not any more. Now
she could roar.

She practised alone at home, found
she could call abroad without using the phone, could sing
like an orchestra in the bath, could yawn like thunder
watching TV. She switched to the News. It was all about
Muslims, Christians, Jews.

Then her scream was a huge bird
that flew her away into the dark; each vast wing a shriek,
awful to hear, the beak the sickening hiss of a thrown spear.
She stayed up there all night, in the wind and rain, wailing,
uttering lightning.

Down, she was pure sound, rumbling
like an avalanche. She bit radios, swallowed them, gargled
their News, till the words were – *ran into the church and sprayed
the congregation with bullets no one has claimed* – gibberish, crap,
in the cave of her mouth.

Her voice stomped through the city,
shouting the odds, shaking the bells awake in their towers.
She yelled through the countryside, swelling the rivers, felling
the woods. She put out to sea, screeching and bellowing,
spewing brine.

She bawled at the moon and it span away
into space. She hollered into the dark where fighter planes
buzzed at her face. She howled till every noise in the world
sang in the spit on the tip of her tongue: the shriek of a bomb,
the bang of a gun,

the prayers of the priest, the pad of the feet
in the mosque, the casual rip of the post, the mothers' sobs,
the thump of the drop, the President's cough, the screams
of the children cowering under their pews, loud, loud,
louder, the News.

History

She woke up old at last, alone,
bones in a bed, not a tooth
in her head, half dead, shuffled
and limped downstairs
in the rag of her nightdress,
smelling of pee.

        Slurped tea, stared
at her hand – twigs, stained gloves –
wheezed and coughed, pulled on
the coat that hung from a hook
on the door, lay on the sofa,
dozed, snored.

        She was History.
She'd seen them ease him down
from the Cross, his mother gasping
for breath, as though his death
was a difficult birth, the soldiers spitting,
spears in the earth;

        been there
when the fishermen swore he was back
from the dead; seen the basilicas rise
in Jerusalem, Constantinople, Sicily; watched
for a hundred years as the air of Rome
turned into stone;

witnessed the wars,
the bloody crusades, knew them by date
and by name, Bannockburn, Passchendaele,
Babi Yar, Vietnam. She'd heard the last words
of the martyrs burnt at the stake, the murderers
hung by the neck,

             seen up-close
how the saint whistled and spat in the flames,
how the dictator strutting on stuttering film
blew out his brains, how the children waved
their little hands from the trains. She woke again,
cold, in the dark,

             in the empty house.
Bricks through the window now, thieves
in the night. When they rang on her bell
there was nobody there; fresh graffiti sprayed
on her door, shit wrapped in a newspaper posted
onto the floor.

Sub

I came on in extra time in '66, my breasts
bandaged beneath my no. 13 shirt, and put it in
off the head, the back of the heel, the left foot
from 30 yards out, hat-trick. If they'd thought
the game was all over, it was now. I felt secure
as I danced in my dazzling whites with the Cup –
tampon – but skipped the team bath with the lads,
sipped my champagne in the solitary shower
as the blood and soap suds mingled to pink.
They sang my name on the other side of the steam.

Came on too in the final gasps of the Grand Slam clincher,
scooped up the ball from the back of the scrum, ran
like the wind, bandaged again, time of the month
likewise, wiggled, weaved, waved at the crowd, slipped
like soap through muddy hands, liked that, slid
between legs, nursing the precious egg of the ball,
then flung myself like breaking surf over the line
for the winning try, converted it, was carried
shoulder high by the boys as the whistle blew.
They roared my name through mouthfuls of broken teeth.

Ringo had flu when the Fab Four toured Down
Under. Minus a drummer, the gig was a bummer
till I stepped in, digits ringed, sticked, skinned,
in a Beatle skirt, mop-topped, fringed, to wink
at Paul, quip with John, climb on the drums,
clever fingered and thumbed, give it four to the bar,
give it *yeah yeah yeah*. The screams were lava,
hot as sex, and every seat in the house was wet.

We sang *Help!*, *Day Tripper, Money, This Boy,*
Girl, She Loves You – John, Paul, George and Moi.

It was one small step for a man for Neil
to stand on the Moon, a small hop for me
to stand in for Buzz, bounce in my moon-suit
over the dust, waving a flag. I knelt, scooped out
a hole in the powdery ground, and buried a box
with a bottle of malt, chocolates, Emily Dickinson's
poems. Ground Control barked down the line. *Houston,*
we don't have a problem, I said. It comforts me now,
the thought of them there, when I look at the moon.
Quietly there on the moon, the things that I like.

And when Beefy fell sick in the final Test,
I stepped up, two of his boxes over my chest,
and hooked a four from the first of Lillee's balls.
He bowled so fast you could hear his fingers click
as he spun off the seam. I lolled at the crease –
five months gone – and looped and hooped them about
like a dream, googlies, bosies, chinamen, zooters,
balls that dipped, flipped, nipped, whipped
at the wicket like bombs. I felt the first kick
of my child; whacked a century into the crowd.

Motherhood then kept me busy at home till my girl
started school. Not match-fit, I was talked
into management when Taylor went, caretaker role,
jacked that in after the World Cup win – Beckham
free-kick in extra time – and agreed on a whim to slim
to the weight of a boy, ride the winner at Aintree –
Bobbyjo, '99 – when the jockey dislocated his neck.
After that, I pulled right back, signed up to write

a book of my life and times, though I did play guitar
for the Band in LA when Bob gave me the call.

And when I look back – or my grandchildren ask me
what it was like to put Mohammed Ali on the deck
when Cooper was scratched from the scrap, or stand in
for Graham Hill to be Formula One Grand Champ
in the fastest recorded speed, or to dress up
as Borg in bandana and wig and steal the fifth set
at Wimbledon from under – *You cannot be serious* –
McEnroe's nose, or to kneel, best of all, first woman there,
on the Moon and gaze at the beautiful faraway earth –
what I think to myself is this:

The Virgin's Memo

maybe not abscesses, acne, asthma,
son, maybe not boils,
maybe not cancer
or diarrhoea
or tinnitus of the inner ear,
maybe not fungus,
maybe rethink the giraffe,
maybe not herpes, son,
or (text illegible)
or jellyfish
or (untranslatable)
maybe not leprosy or lice,
the menopause or mice, mucus, son,
neuralgia, nits,
maybe not body odour,
piles,
quicksand, quagmires,
maybe not rats, son, rabies, rattlesnakes,
shite,
and maybe hang fire on the tarantula,
the unicorn's lovely,
but maybe not veruccas
or wasps,
or (text illegible)
or (untranslatable)
maybe not . . .

Anon

If she were here
she'd forget who she was,
it's been so long,
maybe a nurse, a nanny,
maybe a nun –
Anon.

A girl I met
was willing to bet
that she still lived on –
Anon –
but had packed it all in,
the best verb, the right noun,
for a life in the sun.

A woman I knew
kept her skull
on a shelf in a room –
Anon's –
and swore that one day
as she worked at her desk
it cleared its throat
as though it had something
to get off its chest.

But I know best –
how she passed on her pen
like a baton
down through the years,
with a hey nonny
hey nonny
hey nonny no –
Anon.

The Laughter of Stafford Girls' High

(for T.W.)

It was a girl in the Third Form, Carolann Clare,
who, bored with the lesson, the rivers of England –
Brathay, Coquet, Crake, Dee, Don, Goyt,
Rothay, Tyne, Swale, Tees, Wear, Wharfe . . .
had passed a note, which has never been found,
to the classmate in front, Emily Jane, a girl
who adored the teacher, Miss V. Dunn MA,
steadily squeaking her chalk on the board –
Allen, Clough, Duddon, Feugh, Greta, Hindburn,
Irwell, Kent, Leven, Lowther, Lune, Sprint . . .
but who furtively opened the folded note,
torn from the back of the King James Bible, read
what was scribbled there and laughed out loud.

It was a miserable, lowering winter's day. The girls
had been kept indoors at break – Wet Play
in the Hall – the windows tall and thin,
sad with rain like a long list of watery names –
Rawthey, Roeburn, Skirfare, Troutbeck, Wash . . .
likewise, the sound of the laugh of Emily Jane
was a liquid one, a gurgle, a ripple, a dribble,
a babble, a gargle, a plash, a splash of a laugh
like the sudden jackpot leap of a silver fish
in the purse of a pool. No fool, Emily Jane
clamped her turquoisey hand – her fountain pen leaked –
to her mouth; but the laugh was out, was at large,
was heard by the pupil twinned to her double desk –

Rosemary Beth – the brace on whose jiggly teeth
couldn't restrain the gulping giggle she gave
which caused Miss Dunn to spin round. *Perhaps,*
she said, *We can all share the joke?* But Emily Jane
had scrunched and dropped the note with the joke
to the floor and kicked it across to Jennifer Kay
who snorted and toed it to Marjorie May
who spluttered and heeled it backwards
to Jessica Kate. *Girls!* By now, every girl in the form
had started to snigger or snicker or titter or chuckle
or chortle till the classroom came to the boil
with a brothy mirth. *Girls!* Miss Dunn's shrill voice
scraped Top G and only made matters worse.

Five minutes passed in a cauldron of noise.
No one could seem to stop. Each tried holding
her breath or thinking of death or pinching
her thigh, only to catch the eye of a pal,
a crimson, shaking, silent girl, and explode
through the nose in a cackling sneeze. *Thank you!*
Please! screeched Miss Dunn, clapping her hands
as though she applauded the choir they'd become,
a percussion of trills and whoops filling the room
like birds in a cage. But then came a triple rap
at the door and in stalked Miss Fife, Head of Maths,
whose cold equations of eyes scanned the desks
for a suitable scapegoat. *Stand up, Geraldine Ruth.*

Geraldine Ruth got to her feet, a pale girl, a girl
who looked, in the stale classroom light, like a sketch
for a girl, a first draft to be crumpled and crunched
and tossed away like a note. She cleared her throat,
raising her eyes, water and sky, to look at Miss Fife.

The girls who were there that day never forgot
how invisible crayons seemed to colour in
Geraldine Ruth, white face to puce, mousey hair
suddenly gifted with health and youth, and how –
as Miss Fife demanded what was the meaning of this –
her lips split from the closed bud of a kiss
to the daisy chain of a grin and how then she yodelled
a laugh with the full, open, blooming rose of her throat,

a flower of merriment. *What's the big joke?*
thundered Miss Fife as Miss Dunn began again
to clap, as gargling Geraldine Ruth collapsed
in a heap on her desk, as the rest of the class
hollered and hooted and howled. Miss Fife strode
on sharp heels to the blackboard, snatched up
a finger of chalk and jabbed and slashed out
a word. *SILENCE*. But the class next door,
Fourth Years learning the Beaufort scale with Miss Batt,
could hear the commotion. Miss Batt droned on –
*Nought, calm; one, light air; two, light breeze; three,
gentle . . . four, moderate . . . five, fresh . . . six, strong breeze;
seven, moderate gale . . .* Stephanie Fay started to laugh.

What's so amusing, Stephanie Fay? barked Miss Batt.
What's so amusing? echoed unwitting Miss Dunn
on the other side of the wall. *Precisely what's
so amusing?* chorused Miss Fife. The Fourth Years
shrieked with amazed delight and one wag,
Angela Joy, popped her head in the jaws of her desk
and bellowed *What's so amusing? What's so
amusing?* into its musty yawn. The Third Form
guffawed afresh at the sound of the Fourth
and the noise of the two combined was heard
by the First Form, trying to get Shakespeare by heart

to the beat of the ruler of Mrs Mackay. *Don't look
at your books, look at me. After three. Friends,*

Romans, Countrymen . . . What's so amusing? rapped out
Mrs Mackay as the First Years chirruped
and trilled like baby birds in a nest at a worm;
but she heard for herself, appalled, the chaos
coming in waves through the wall and clipped
to the door. Uproar. And her Head of Lower School!
It was then that Mrs Mackay made mistake number one,
leaving her form on its own while she went to see
to the forms of Miss Batt and Miss Dunn. The moment
she'd gone, the room blossomed with paper planes,
ink bombs, whistles, snatches of song, and the class clown –
Caroline Joan – stood on her desk and took up
the speech where Mrs Mackay had left off – *Lend*

me your ears . . . just what the Second Form did
in the opposite room, reciting the Poets Laureate
for Miss Nadimbaba – *John Dryden, Thomas Shadwell,
Nahum Tate, Nicholas Rowe, Laurence Eusden, Colley Cibber,
William Whitehead . . .* but scattering titters and giggles
like noisy confetti on reaching Henry Pye as Caroline Joan
belted out Antony's speech in an Elvis style –
For Brutus, uh huh huh, is an honourable man.
Miss Nadimbaba, no fan of rock 'n' roll, could scarcely
believe her ears, deducing at once that Mrs Mackay
was not with her class. She popped an anxious head
outside her door. Anarchy roared in her face
like a tropical wind. The corridor clock was at four.

The last bell rang. Although they would later regret it,
the teachers, taking their cue from wits-end Mrs Mackay,
allowed the chuckling, bright-eyed, mirthful girls

to go home, reprimand-free, each woman privately glad
that the dark afternoon was over and done,
the chalky words rubbed away to dance as dust
on the air, the dates, the battles, the kings and queens,
the rivers and tributaries, poets, painters, playwrights,
politicos, popes . . . but they all agreed to make it quite clear
in tomorrow's Assembly that foolish behaviour –
even if only the once – wasn't admired or desired
at Stafford Girls' High. Above the school, the moon
was pinned like a monitor's badge to the sky.

Miss Dunn was the first to depart, wheeling
her bicycle through the gates, noticing how
the sky had cleared, a tidy diagram of the Plough
directly above. She liked it this cold, her breath
chiffoning out behind as she freewheeled home
down the hill, her mind emptying itself of geography,
of mountains and seas and deserts and forests
and capital cities. Her small terraced house looked,
she thought, like a sleeping face. She roused it
each evening, kisses of light on its cheeks
from her lamps, the small talk of cutlery, pots
and pans as she cooked, sweet silver steam caressing
the shy rooms of her home. Miss Dunn lived alone.

So did Miss Batt, in a flat on the edge of the park
near the school; though this evening Miss Fife
was coming for supper. The two were good friends
and Miss Fife liked to play on Miss Batt's small piano
after the meal and the slowly shared carafe of wine.
Music and Maths! Johann Sebastian Bach! Miss Batt,
an all-rounder, took out her marking – essays on Henry VIII
and his wives from the Fifth – while Miss Fife gave herself up
to Minuet in G. In between Catherine Howard

and Catherine Parr, Miss Batt glanced across at Fifi's
straight back as she played, each teacher conscious
of each woman's silently virtuous love. Nights like this,
twice a week, after school, for them both, seemed enough.

Mrs Mackay often gave Miss Nadimbaba a lift,
as they both, by coincidence, lived on Mulberry Drive –
Mrs Mackay with her husband of twenty-five grinding,
childless years; Miss Nadimbaba sharing a house
with her elderly aunt. Neither had ever invited
the other one in, although each would politely enquire
after her colleague's invisible half. Mrs Mackay
watched Miss Nadimbaba open her purple door and saw
a cat rubbing itself on her calf. She pulled away
from the kerb, worrying whether Mr Mackay would insist
on fish for his meal. Then he would do his crossword:
Mr Mackay calling out clues – *Kind of court for a bounder (8)* –
while she passed him *Roget, Brewer, Pears,* the *OED.*

The women teachers of England slept in their beds,
their shrewd or wise or sensible heads safe vessels
for Othello's jealousy, the Wife of Bath's warm laugh,
the phases of the moon, the country code;
for Roman numerals, Greek alphabets, French verbs;
for foreign currencies and Latin roots, for logarithms, tables,
quotes; the meanings of *currente calamo* and *fiat lux* and *stet.*
Miss Dunn dreamed of a freezing white terrain
where slowly moving elephants were made of ice.
Miss Nadimbaba dreamed she knelt to kiss Miss Barrett
on her couch and she, Miss Nadimbaba, was Browning
saying *Beloved, be my wife* . . . and then a dog began to bark
and she woke up. Miss Batt dreamed of Miss Fife.

*   *   *

Morning assembly – the world like Quink outside,
the teachers perched in a solemn row on the stage,
the Fifth and Sixth Forms clever and tall, Miss Fife
at the school piano, the Head herself, Doctor Bream,
at the stand – was a serious affair. *Jerusalem* hung
in the air till the last of Miss Fife's big chords
wobbled away. *Yesterday*, intoned Doctor Bream,
the Lower School behaved in a foolish way, sniggering
for most of the late afternoon. She glared at the girls
through her pince-nez and paused for dramatic effect.
But the First and Second and Third and Fourth Forms
started to laugh, each girl trying to swallow it down
till the sound was like distant thunder, the opening chord

of a storm. Miss Dunn and Miss Batt, Miss Nadimbaba
and Mrs Mackay leapt to their feet as one, grim-faced.
The Fifth Form hooted and howled. Miss Fife, oddly disturbed,
crashed down fistfuls of furious notes on the yellowing keys.
The Sixth Forms, upper and lower, shrieked. Señora Devizes,
sartorial, strict, slim, severe, teacher of Spanish,
stalked from the stage and stilettoed sharply down
to the back of the Hall to chastise the Fifth and Sixth.
¡Callaos! ¡Callaos! ¡Callaos! ¡Quédense! The whole school
guffawed; their pink young lungs flowering more
than they had for the hymn. *¡El clamor!* The Hall was a zoo.
Snow began falling outside as though the clouds
were being slowly torn up like a rule book. *A good laugh,*

as the poet Ursula Fleur, who attended the school,
was to famously write, *is feasting on air.* The air that day
was chomped, chewed, bitten in two, pulled apart
like a wishbone, licked like a lollipop, sluiced and sucked.
Some of the girls were almost sick. Girls gulped or sipped
or slurped as they savoured the joke. What joke?

Nobody knew. A silly joy sparkled and fizzed. Tabitha Rose,
flower monitor for the day, wet herself, wailed, wept, ran
from the Hall, a small human shower of rain. The bell
for the start of lessons rang. Somehow the school
filed out in a raggedy line. The Head Girl, Josephine June,
scarlet-faced from killing herself, was in for a terrible time
with the Head. Snow iced the school like a giant cake.

No one on record recalls the words that were said,
but Josephine June was stripped of the Head Girl's badge
and sash and sent to the Sixth Form Common Room
to demand of the prefects how they could hope to grow to be
the finest of England's daughters and mothers and wives
after this morning's Assembly's abysmal affair?
But the crowd of girls gave a massive cheer, stamping
the floor with their feet in a rebel beat and Diana Kim,
Captain of Sports, jumped on a chair and declared
that if J.J. was no longer Head Girl then no one
would take her place. *All for one!* someone yelled. *And one
for all!* Diana Kim opened the window and jumped down
into the snow. With a shriek, Emmeline Belle jumped after her,

followed by cackling Anthea Meg, Melanie Hope, Andrea Lyn,
J.J. herself . . . It was Gillian Tess in the Fifth, being lectured
by tight-lipped Señora Devizes on how to behave, who glanced
from the first-floor window and noticed the Sixth Form
bouncing around in the snow like girls on the moon.
A snowball, the size of a netball, was creaking, rolling,
growing under their hands. *Look!* Girls at their windows gaped.
It grew from a ball to the size of a classroom globe. It grew
from a globe to the size of a huge balloon. Miss Dunn,
drumming the world's highest mountains into the heads
of the First Years – *Everest, K2, Kangchenjunga, Lhoste, Makalu 1* . . .

flung open her window and breathed in the passionate cold
of the snow. A wild thought seeded itself in her head.

In later years, the size of the snowball rolled by the Sixth
grew like a legend. Some claimed that the Head, as it groaned
past her study, thought that there might have been an eclipse.
Ursula Fleur, in her prose poem *Snow*, wrote that it took
the rest of the Michaelmas Term to melt. Miss Batt,
vacantly staring down as her class wrote out a list
of the monarchs of England – *Egbert, Ethelwulf, Ethelbald,
Ethelbert, Ethelred, Alfred, Edward, Athelstan, Edmund,
Eadred, Eadwig, Edgar* . . . noticed the snowball, huge and alone
on the hockey pitch, startlingly white in the pencilly grey
of the light, and thought of desire, of piano scales slowing,
slowing, breasts. She moaned aloud, forgetful of where
she was. Francesca Eve echoed the moan. The class roared.

But that night Miss Batt, while she cooked for Miss Fife,
who was opening the wine with a corkscrew
from last year's school trip to Sienna and Florence,
felt herself naked, electric under her tartan skirt, twin set
and pearls; and later, Miss Fife at the piano, stroking
the first notes of Beethoven's 'Moonlight' Sonata, Miss Batt
came behind her, placing her inked and trembling hands
on her shoulders. A broken A minor chord stumbled
and died. Miss Fife said that Ludwig could only
have written this piece when he was in love. Miss Batt
pulled Miss Fife by the hair, turning her face around, hearing
her gasp, bending down, kissing her, kissing her, kissing her.
Essays on Cardinal Wolsey lay unmarked on the floor.

Across the hushed white park, down the slush of the hill,
Miss Dunn crouched on the floor of her sitting room
over a map of Tibet. The whisky glass in her nervous hand

clunked on her teeth, Talisker sheathing her tongue
in a heroine's warmth. She moved her finger slowly
over the map, the roof of the world. Her fingers walked to Nepal,
changing the mountain *Chomolungma* to *Sagarmatha*.
She sipped at her malt and thought about Mallory, lost
on Everest's slopes with his English Air, of how he'd wanted
to reach the summit *because it was there*. She wondered
whether he had. Nobody knew. She saw herself walking
the upper slopes with the Captain of Sports towards
the foetal shape of a sleeping man . . . She turned to the girl.

*   *   *

That Monday morning Doctor Bream, at her desk,
didn't yet know that the laughter of Stafford Girls' High
would not go away. But when she stood on the stage,
garbed in her Cambridge cap and gown, and told the school
to quietly stand and contemplate a fresh and serious start
to the week, and closed her eyes – the hush like an air balloon
tethered with ropes – a low and vulgar giggle yanked
at the silence. Doctor Bream kept her eyes clenched, hoping
that if she ignored it all would be well. Clumps of laughter
sprouted among the row upon row of girls. Doctor Bream,
determined and blind, started the morning's hymn. *I vow
to thee my country* . . . A flushed Miss Fife started to play.
All earthly things above . . . The rest of the staff joined in –

*entire and whole and perfect, the service of my love,
the love that asks no questions, the love that stands the test* . . .
But the girls were hysterical, watching the Head,
Queen Canute, singing against the tide of their mirth,
their shoals, their glittering laughter. She opened her eyes –
Clarice Maud Bream, MBE, DLitt – and saw, in the giggling sea
one face which seemed to her to be worse, cheekier,

redder and louder, than all of the rest. Nigella Dawn
was fished by the Head from her seat and made to stand
on a chair on the stage. Laughter drained from the Hall. *This girl,*
boomed the Head, *will stand on this chair for as long as it takes
for the school to come to its senses. SILENCE!* The whole school
stood like a crowd waiting for news. The bell rang. Nobody

moved. Nobody made a sound. Minutes slinked away
as Nigella Dawn swayed on her creaky chair. The First Years
stared in shame at their shoes. The Head's tight smile
was a tick. *That,* she thought, in a phrase of her mother's,
has put the tin lid on that. A thin high whine, a kitten,
wind on a wire, came from behind. The school
seemed to hold its breath. Nigella Dawn shook on her chair.
The sound came again, louder. Doctor Bream looked to the staff.
Miss Batt had her head in her lap and was keening and rocking
backwards and forwards. The noise put the Head in mind
of a radio dial – *Luxembourg, Light, Hilversum, Welsh* –
as though the woman were trying to tune in to herself. Miss Batt
flung her head back and laughed, laughed like a bride.

*   *   *

Mr and Mrs Mackay silently ate. She eyed him
boning his fish, slicing it down to the backbone,
sliding the skeleton out, fastidious, deft. She spied him
eat from the right of his plate to the left, ordered, precise.
She clenched herself for his voice. *A very nice dish
from the bottomless deep.* Bad words ran in her head like mice.
She wanted to write them down in the crossword lights.
14 Across: *F* . . . 17 Down: *F* . . . . . . 2 Down: *F* . . . . . .
Mr Mackay reached for the OED. She bit her lip. *A word
for one who is given to walking by night, not necessarily
in sleep.* She felt her heart flare in its dark cave, hungry, blind,

open its small beak. *Beginning with* N. Mrs Mackay
moved to the window and stared at the ravenous night. Later,

awake in the beached boat of the marital bed, Mrs Mackay
slid from between the sheets. Her spouse whistled and whined.
She dressed in sweater and slacks, in boots, in her old tweed coat,
and slipped from the house with a tut of the front door snib.
Her breath swaggered away like a genie popped from a flask.
She looked for the moon, found it, arched high over the house,
a raised eyebrow of light, and started to walk. The streets
were empty, darkly sparkling under her feet, ribbons that tied
the sleeping town like a gift. A black cat glared from a wall.
Mrs Mackay walked and walked and walked, letting the night
sigh underneath her clothes, perfume her skin; letting it in,
the scented night – stone, starlight, tree-sleep, rat, owl.
A calm rhythm measured itself in her head. *Noctambulist.*

She walked for hours, till dawn's soft tip rubbed, smudged,
erased the dark. Back home, she stripped and washed
and dressed for school, moving about in the kitchen
till Mr Mackay appeared, requesting a four-minute egg
from a satisfied hen. She watched him slice off the top
with the side of his spoon, dip in his toast, savour the soft gold
of the yolk with his neat tongue. She thought of the girls,
how they'd laughed now for weeks. Panic nipped and salted
her eyes. And later that day, walking among the giggling desks
of the Third, she read Cleopatra's lament in a shaking voice
as tears shone on her cheeks: *Hast thou no care of me?*
Shall I abide in this dull world, which in thy absence is
No better than a sty? O! see my women, the crown

o' the earth doth melt. My lord! O! withered is the garland
of the war, the soldier's pole is fall'n; young boys and girls
are level now with men; the odds is gone, and there is nothing

left remarkable beneath the visiting moon. Carolann Clare, trapped
in a breathless, crippling laugh, seriously thought she would die.
Mrs Mackay lay down her book and asked the girls to start
from the top and carry on reading the play round the class.
She closed her eyes and seemed to drift off at her desk.
The voices of girls shared Shakespeare, line by line, the clock
over the blackboard crumbling its minutes into the dusty air.
From the other side of the wall, light breezes of laughter came
and went. Further away, from the music room, the sound
of the orchestra hooted and sneered its way through Grieg.

Miss Batt, in the staffroom, marking The War of Jenkins' Ear
over and over again, put down her pen. Music reminded her
of Miss Fife. She lay her head on the table, dizzy with lust, longed
for the four o'clock bell, for home, for pasta and *vino rosso*,
for Fifi's body on hers in the single bed, for kisses that tasted
of jotters, of wine. She picked up an essay and read:
*England went to war with Spain because a seaman, Robert
Jenkins, claimed that the Spanish thought him a smuggler
and cut off his ear. He showed the ear in the Commons
and public opinion forced the Government to declare war
on October 23, 1739 . . .* Miss Batt cursed under her breath,
slashing a red tick with her pen. The music had stopped. Hilarity
squealed and screeched in its place down the corridor.

Miss Nadimbaba was teaching the poems of Yeats
to the Fifth when the girls in the orchestra laughed. She held
in her hands the poem which had made her a scribbler of verse
at twelve or thirteen. 'The Song' – she was sick of the laughter
at Stafford Girls' High – 'of Wandering Aengus.' She stared
at the girls in her class who were starting to shake. An epidemic,
that's what it was. It had gone on all term. It was now the air
that they breathed, teachers and girls: a giggling, sniggering,
gurgling, snickering atmosphere, a laughing gas that seeped

under doors, up corridors, into the gym, the chemistry lab,
the swimming pool, into Latin and Spanish and French and Greek,
into Needlework, History, Art, R.K., P.E., into cross-country runs,
into the silver apples of the moon, the golden apples of the sun.

Miss Dunn stood with her bike outside school after four,
scanning the silly, cackling girls for a face – Diana Kim's.
The Captain of Sports was tall, red-haired. Her green eyes
stared at Miss Dunn and Miss Dunn *knew*. This was a girl
who would scale a vertical wall of ice with her fingertips,
who would pitch a tent on the lip of a precipice, who would know
when the light was good, when the wind was bad, when snow
was powdery or hard. The girl had the stuff of heroines. Diana Kim
walked with the teacher, pushing her bicycle for her, hearing her
outline the journey, the great adventure, the climb to the Mother
of Earth. Something inside her opened and bloomed.
Miss Dunn was her destiny, fame, a strong hand pulling her
higher and higher into the far Tibetan clouds, into the sun.

*   *   *

Doctor Bream was well aware that something had to be done.
Laughter, it seemed, was on the curriculum. The girls
found everything funny, strange; howled or screamed
at the slightest thing. The Headmistress prowled the school,
listening at classroom doors. The new teacher, Mrs Munro,
was reading The Flaying of Marsyas to the Third: *Help!*
Why are you stripping me from myself? The girls were in fits.
Mrs Munro's tight voice struggled on: *It was possible to count*
his throbbing organs and the chambers of his lungs. Shrieks
and squeals stabbed the air. Why? At what? Doctor Bream
snooped on. Miss Batt was teaching the First Form the names
of the nine major planets: *Mercury, Venus, Earth, Mars,*
Jupiter, Saturn, Uranus . . . Pandemonium hooted and whooped.

The grim Head passed down the corridor, hearing the Fifth Form
gargling its way through the Diet of Worms. She came
to the Honours Board, the names of the old girls written in gold –
Head Girls who had passed into legend, Captains of Sport
who had played the game, prize-winning girls, girls who'd gone on
to achieve great things. Members of Parliament! Blasts of laughter
belched from the playing fields. Doctor Bream walked to her room
and stood by her desk. Her certificates preened behind glass
in the wintery light. Silver medals and trophies and cups gleamed
in the cabinet. She went to the wall – the school photograph
glinted and glowed, each face like a fingertip; the pupils
straight-backed, straight-faced; the staff upright, straight-laced.
A warm giggle burbled outside. She flung open the door.

The empty corridor winked. She could hear
a distant piano practising Für Elise . . . Señora Devizes
counting in Spanish in one of the rooms – *uno, dos, tres,*
cuatro, cinco, seis, siete, ocho, nueve, diez, once, doce,
trece, catorce, quince, diez y seis, diez y siete, diez y ocho . . .
a shrill whistle blowing outside . . . But then a burst of hysteria
came from the classroom above, rolled down the stairs,
exploded again in the classroom below. Mrs Mackay,
frantic, hoarse, could be heard pitching Portia's speech
over the hoots of the Fourth: *The quality of MERCY*
is not STRAINED. It droppeth as the gentle rain from HEAVEN
upon the place BENEATH . . . Cackles, like gunfire, crackled
and spat through the school. A cheer boomed from the Gym.

It went on thus – through every hymn or poem, catechism,
logarithm, sum, exam; in every classroom, drama room
to music room; on school trips to a factory or farm; from
First to Sixth Form, dunce to academic crème de la crème,
day in, day out; till, towards the end of the Hilary Term,

Doctor Bream called yet another meeting in the Staffroom,
determined now to solve the problem of the laughter
of the girls once and for all. The staff filed in at 4.15 –
Miss Batt, Miss Fife, Miss Dunn, Mrs Munro, the sporty
Mrs Lee, Mrs Mackay, Miss Nadimbaba, the Heads of French
and Science – Miss Feaver, Mrs Kaye – Señora Devizes,
the tuneful Miss Aherne, the part-time drama teacher
Mrs Prendergast. The Head stood up and clapped her hands.

Miss Fife poured Earl Grey tea. Miss Dunn stood by the window,
staring out. Miss Batt burned at Miss Fife. Mrs Mackay
sat down and closed her eyes. Miss Nadimbaba churned
the closing couplet of a poem in her head. Miss Feaver
crossed her legs and smiled at Mrs Lee, who twirled
a squash racquet between her rosy knees. *I think we all agree,*
said Doctor Bream, *that things are past the pale. The girls
are learning nothing. Discipline's completely gone
to pot. I'd like to hear from each of you in turn. Mrs Mackay?*
Mrs Mackay opened her eyes and sighed. And shook her head.
And then she started singing: *It was a lover and his lass,
with a hey, and a ho, and a hey nonino, that o'er
the green cornfield did pass, in the spring time,*

*the only pretty ring time, when birds do sing, hey ding
a ding, ding; sweet lovers love the spring.* A silence fell.
Miss Batt looked at Miss Fife and cleared her throat. *Miss Fife
and I are leaving at the end of term.* Miss Dunn at the window
turned. *I'm leaving then myself. To have a crack at Everest . . .*
The Head sank to a chair. Miss Nadimbaba stood. Then one by one
the staff resigned – to publish poetry, to live in Spain, to form
a tennis club, to run a restaurant in Nice, to tread the boards,
to sing in smoky clubs, to translate Ovid into current speech,
to study homeopathy. Doctor Bream was white with shock.

And what, she forced herself at last to say, *about the girls?*
Miss Batt, slowly undressing Fifi in the stockroom in her head,
winked at Miss Fife. She giggled girlishly. Miss Feaver laughed.

* * *

Small hours. The moon tracked Mrs Mackay as she reached the edge
of the sleeping town, houses dwindling to fields, the road
twisting up and away into the distant hills. She caught her mind
making anagrams – *grow heed, stab, rats* – and forced herself
to chant aloud as she walked. Hedgerow. Bats. Star. Her head
cleared. The town was below her now, dark and hunched,
a giant husband bunched in his sleep. Mrs Mackay climbed on,
higher and higher, keeping close to the ditch, till the road snaked
in a long S then levelled out into open countryside. *Shore,*
love, steer, low, master, night loom, riven use, no. Horse. Vole.
Trees. Owl. Stream. Moonlight. Universe. On. *Wed, loop, wand,*
drib, tiles, pay thaw, god. Dew. Pool. Dawn. Bird. Stile. Pathway.
Dog. She arrived at the fringe of a village as morning broke.

Miss Batt held Miss Fife in her arms at dawn, the small room
chaste with new light. Miss Fife began to talk in her sleep –
The square on the hypotenuse is equal to the sum
of the squares of the other two sides. Miss Batt slid down,
nuzzled her breastbone, her stomach, kissed down,
kissed down, down to the triangle. The tutting bedside clock
counted to five. They woke again at seven, stupid with love,
everything they knew – the brightest stars, Sirius, Canopus,
Alpha Centauri, Vega; the Roman Emperors, Claudius,
Nero, Galba, Otho, Vitellius; musical terms, *allegro, calando,*
crescendo, glissando; mathematics, the value of pi,
prime numbers, Cantor's infinities – only a jumble of words,
a jumble of words. A long deep zero groaned from Miss Fife.

Miss Dunn took out her list and checked it again. Her class
was sniggering its way through a test on Britain's largest lakes.
She mouthed her list like a prayer: socks, mittens, shirt, leggings,
hat, face mask, goggles, harness, karabiners, ice screws, pitons,
helmet, descender, ascender, loops, slings, ice axe, gaiters,
crampons, boots, jacket, hood, trousers, water bottle, urine
bottle, waste bags, sleeping bag, kit bag, head torch, batteries,
tent, medical kit, maps, stove, butane, radio, fixing line, rope,
cord, stoppers, wands, stakes and chocks and all of it twice.
A sprinkle of giggles made her look up. *Pass your test to the girl
on your left to be marked. The answers are: Lough Neagh,
Lower Lough Erne, Loch Lomond, Loch Ness, Loch Awe, Upper
Lough Erne . . .* Diana Kim climbed and climbed in her head.

Doctor Bream read through the letter to parents then signed
her name at the end. The school was to close at the end of term
until further notice. A dozen resignation notes from the staff
lay on her desk. The Head put her head in her hands and wept.
A local journalist lurked at the gates. Señora Devizes
and Miss Nadimbaba entered the room to say that the girls
were filing into the Hall for the Special Assembly. There was still
no sign of Mrs Mackay. She looked at the shattered Head
and Kipling sprang to Miss Nadimbaba's lips: *If you can force
your heart and nerve and sinew to serve your turn long after they
are gone . . .* Señora Devizes joined in: *Persiste aun no tengas
fuerza, y sólo te quede la voluntad que les dice:
¡Persiste!* The Head got to her feet and straightened her back.

And so, Doctor Bream summed up, *you girls have laughed this once
great school into the ground. Señora Devizes plans to return
to Spain.* Cries of *¡Olé! Miss Batt and Miss Fife have resigned.*
Wolf whistles. *Mrs Prendergast is joining the Theatre Royale.*
A round of applause crashed on the boards like surf. The Head stared
at the laughing girls then turned and marched from the stage,

clipped up the polished corridor, banged through the double doors,
crunched down the gravel drive to the Staff Car Park and into her car.
Elvis, shrieked Caroline Joan from the Hall, *has left the building.*
A cheer like an avalanche bounced off the roof. The Captain of Sports
slipped from her seat and followed Miss Dunn. The girls burst
into song as their mute teachers walked from the stage. *Till we
have built Jerusalem in England's green and pleasant land.*

* * *

The empty school creaked and sighed, its desks the small coffins
of lessons, its blackboards the tombstones of learning. The books
in the Library stiffened and yellowed and curled. The portraits
of gone Headmistresses stared into space. The school groaned,
the tiles on its roof falling off in its sleep, its windows as white
as chalk. The grass on the playing fields grew like grass
on a grave. Doctor Bream stared from her hospital window
over the fields. She could see the school bell in its tower glint
in the evening sun like a tear in an eye. She turned away. Postcards
and get-well messages from the staff were pinned to the wall.
She took down a picture of Everest from Miss Dunn: *We leave
Camp II tomorrow if the weather holds to climb the Corridor
to 21,000 feet. Both coping well with altitude. The Sherpas . . .*

Mrs Mackay walked through Glen Strathfarrar, mad, muttering,
free; a filthy old pack on her back filled with scavenged loot –
banana, bottle, blanket, balaclava, bread, blade, bible. She sat
by a stream, filled her bottle and drank. She ate the crusts,
the fruit. Kingfisher. Eagle. Heron. Red deer. Midge. The Glen
darkened and cooled like History. Mrs Mackay lay in the heather
under her blanket, mumbling lines from Lear: *As mad as the vex'd
sea; singing aloud; crowned with rank fumitor and furrow weeds,
with burdocks, hemlocks, nettles, cuckoo-flowers, darnel . . .*
Syllables. Syllables. Sleep came suddenly, under the huge black,

the chuckling clever stars. The Head at her window looked north
to the clear night sky, to Pollux and Castor, Capella, Polaris,
and wondered again what could have become of Mrs Mackay.

Rough lads from the town came up to the school to throw stones
through the glass. Miss Batt and Miss Fife had moved
to a city. They drank in a dark bar where women danced, cheek
to cheek. Miss Batt loved Miss Fife till she sobbed and shook
in her arms. Stray cats prowled through the classrooms, lunging
at mice. Miss Fife dreamed that the school was a huge ship
floating away from land, all hands lost, steered by a ghost,
a woman whose face was the Head's, was Miss Nadimbaba's,
then Mrs Mackay's, Mrs Lee's, Miss Feaver's, Miss Dunn's,
Mrs Munro's, Mrs Kaye's, Miss Aherne's, Señora Devizes' . . .
She woke in the darkness, a face over hers, a warm mouth
kissing the gibberish from her lips. The school sank in her mind,
a black wave taking it down as she gazed at the woman's face.

Miss Nadimbaba put down her pen and read through her poem.
The palms of her hands felt light, that talented ache. She altered
a verb and the line jumped on the page like a hooked fish. She needed
to type it up, but the poem was done. She was dying
to read it aloud to her aunt. She would open some wine.
In the hospital, a nurse brought warm milk and a pill to the Head,
who stared through the bars at the blackened hulk of the school.
By dawn, at John O'Groats, Mrs Mackay had finally run out of land.
She wrote her maiden name with a stick in the sand then walked
into the sea, steady at first, step by step, till the firm waves lifted her
under her arms and danced her away like a groom with a bride.
High above in the cold sky the seagulls, like schoolgirls, laughed.
Higher again, a teacher fell through the clouds with a girl in her arms.

A Dreaming Week

Not tonight, I'm dreaming
in the heart of the honeyed dark
in a boat of a bed in the attic room
in a house on the edge of the park
where the wind in the big old trees
creaks like an ark.

Not tomorrow, I'm dreaming
till dusk turns into dawn – *dust, must,
most, moot, moon, mown, down* –
with my hand on an open unread book,
a bird that's never flown . . . distantly
the birdsong of the telephone.

Not the following evening, I'm dreaming
in the monocle of the moon,
a sleeping *S* on the page of a bed
in the tome of a dim room, the rain
on the roof, rhyming there,
like the typed words of a poem.

Not the night after that, I'm dreaming
till the stars are blue in the face
printing the news of their old light
with the ink of space,
yards and yards of black silk night
to cover my sleeping face.

Not the next evening, I'm dreaming
in the crook of midnight's arm
like a lover held by another
safe from harm, like a child
stilled by a mother, soft and warm,
twelve golden faraway bells for a charm.

Not that night either, I'm dreaming
till the tides have come and gone
sighing over the frowning sand,
the whale's lonely song
scored on wave after wave of water
all the wet night long.

Not the last evening, I'm dreaming
under the stuttering clock,
under the covers, under closed eyes,
all colours fading to black,
the last of daylight hurrying
for a date with the glamorous dark.

White Writing

No vows written to wed you,
I write them white,
my lips on yours,
light in the soft hours of our married years.

No prayers written to bless you,
I write them white,
your soul a flame,
bright in the window of your maiden name.

No laws written to guard you,
I write them white,
your hand in mine,
palm against palm, lifeline, heartline.

No rules written to guide you,
I write them white,
words on the wind,
traced with a stick where we walk on the sand.

No news written to tell you,
I write it white,
foam on a wave
as we lift up our skirts in the sea, wade,

see last gold sun behind clouds,
inked water in moonlight.
No poems written to praise you,
I write them white.

Gambler

She goes for the sound of the words, the beauty they hold
in the movement they make on the air, the shape
of the breath of a word leaving her lips like a whistle

or kiss. So Hyperion's tips mean nothing to her, the form,
the favourites, whether the going is heavy or firm,
the horse a stinker or first-time blinkered. It's words

she picks, names she ticks. That day it was *Level Headed*
at 10-1, two syllables each to balance the musical chime
of *lev* and *head*, the echoing *el*. She backed it to win

and then on a whim went for *Indian Nectar* at 7-2
to come in next. *Indiannectar. Indiannectar.* She stood
in a trance at the counter, singing it over and over

again in her head which was why, she guessed, she decided
to pick *Sharp Spice* (5-2 fav) to gallop in third – the words
seemed to fit. Most days she sits with her stump of a pen

writing the poems of bets. And how can she lose? Just listen
to some of the names that she didn't choose – *Heiress of Meath,
Springfieldsupreme, Mavis, Shush, Birth of the Blues.*

The Light Gatherer

When you were small, your cupped palms
each held a candlesworth under the skin,
enough light to begin,

                 and as you grew
light gathered in you, two clear raindrops
in your eyes,

           warm pearls, shy,
in the lobes of your ears, even always
the light of a smile after your tears.

Your kissed feet glowed in my one hand,
or I'd enter a room to see the corner you played in
lit like a stage set,

              the crown of your bowed head spotlit.
When language came, it glittered like a river,
silver, clever with fish,

              and you slept
with the whole moon held in your arms for a night light
where I knelt watching.

              Light gatherer. You fell from a star
into my lap, the soft lamp at the bedside
mirrored in you,

and now you shine like a snowgirl,
a buttercup under a chin, the wide blue yonder
you squeal at and fly in,

like a jewelled cave,
turquoise and diamond and gold, opening out
at the end of a tunnel of years.

The Cord

(for Ella)

They cut the cord she was born with
and buried it under a tree
in the heart of the Great Forest
when she was exactly the length
of her mother's nursing elbow
to the tip of her thumb.

She learned to speak and asked them,
though she was young yet,
what the cord had looked like –
had a princess spun it
from a golden spinning wheel?
Could the cord be silver? Was it real?

Real enough and hidden
in the roots of an ancient oak,
the tangled knot of a riddle
or the weird ribbon of a gift
in a poke. As she grew, she asked again
if the cord was made of rope,

then stared from the house she lived in
across the fields to the woods
where rooks spread their pages of wings
like black unreadable books
and the wind in the grass
scribbled sentences wherever she looked.

So she went on foot to the forest
and pressed her ear to the ground,
but not a sound or a movement,
not a breath or a word
gave her a hint where she should go
to hunt for her cord. She went deeper

into the forest, following a bird
which disappeared, a waving hand; shadows
blurred into one huge darkness,
but the stars were her mother's eyes
and the screech of an owl in the tree above
was the sound of a baby's cry.

Wish

But what if, in the clammy soil, her limbs
grew warmer, shifted, stirred, kicked off
the covering of earth, the drowsing corms,
the sly worms, what if her arms reached out
to grab the stone, the grooves of her dates
under her thumb, and pulled her up? I wish.
Her bare feet walk along the gravel path
between the graves, her shroud like washing
blown onto the grass, the petals of her wreath
kissed for a bride. Nobody died. Nobody
wept. Nobody slept who couldn't be woken
by the light. If I can only push open this heavy door
she'll be standing there in the sun, dirty, tired,
wondering why do I shout, why do I run.

North-West

However it is we return to the water's edge
where the ferry grieves down by the Pier Head,
we do what we always did and get on board.
The city drifts out of reach. A huge silvery bird,
a kiss on the lip of the wind, follows our ship.
This is where we were young, the place no map
or heritage guide can reveal. Only an X on a wave
marks the spot, the flowers of litter, a grave
for our ruined loves, unborn children, ghosts.
We look back at the skyline wondering what we lost
in the hidden streets, in the rented rooms,
no more than punters now in a tourist boom.
Above our heads the gulls cry *yeah yeah yeah*.
Frets of light on the river. Tearful air.

Death and the Moon

(for Catherine Marcangeli)

The moon is nearer than where death took you
at the end of the old year. Cold as cash
in the sky's dark pocket, its hard old face
is gold as a mask tonight. I break the ice
over the fish in my frozen pond, look up
as the ghosts of my wordless breath reach
for the stars. If I stood on the tip of my toes
and stretched, I could touch the edge of the moon.

I stooped at the lip of your open grave
to gather a fistful of earth, hard rain,
tough confetti, and tossed it down. It stuttered
like morse on the wood over your eyes, your tongue,
your soundless ears. Then as I slept my living sleep
the ground gulped you, swallowed you whole,
and though I was there when you died,
in the red cave of your widow's unbearable cry,

and measured the space between last words
and silence, I cannot say where you are. Unreachable
by prayer, even if poems are prayers. Unseeable
in the air, even if souls are stars. I turn
to the house, its windows tender with light, the moon,
surely, only as far again as the roof. The goldfish
are tongues in the water's mouth. The black night
is huge, mute, and you are further forever than that.

A Note About the Author

Carol Ann Duffy was born in Glasgow in 1955. She grew up in Stafford and then attended the University of Liverpool, where she received an honors degree in philosophy in 1977. Her poetry publications have received many awards, including both the Forward Prize and the Whitbread Poetry Award for *Mean Time*, as well as the Lannan Literary Award and the E. M. Forster Prize. She has also written two volumes of poetry for children. A Fellow of the Royal Society of Literature, Duffy lives in Manchester, England, where she is Professor of Contemporary Poetry at Manchester Metropolitan University.